Loyalty Management

Typeset in Garamond MT, printed in Canada
by The Coach House Printing Company,
Toronto, Ontario

The publishers gratefully acknowledge the support of the
Canada Council for the Arts and the Ontario Arts Council
for their financial assistance.

Wolsak and Wynn Publishers Ltd
69 Hughson Street North, Ste. 102
Hamilton, ON
Canada L8R 1G5
www.wolsakandwynn.ca

National Library of Canada Cataloguing in Publication Data

Downie, Glen,
        Loyalty management / Glen Downie.

Poems.
ISBN 978-1-894987-16-5

    1. Loyalty – Poetry   I. Title
PS8557.O84L69 2007   C811'.54   C2007-900308-7

for Dale & Emma, finally,
and to the memory of my father

Everything the dead predicted has turned out completely different.
Or a little bit different – which is to say, completely different.
                                        – Wisława Szymborska

Contents

Let the sun never fall into the hands of government

A dream, a wake

Prologue

Purgatorial

Slogging in spring
cross a bogfield—

snow-amnesty
retracted

all lies revealed   shirked
shit   neglected
news   poorly-loved
gloves—

it was then a swallow squadron
started ringing me
chest high

staging a tiny air show
round my heart

I could only marvel
& laugh

I know now
that was God

circling my name on a list
saying
He's ready

Brick talking about brick

Fafard's cows take Toronto

Let there be cows!
beneath the CN Tower

heaps of cud-chewing cows
blocking access to Eaton Centre

meandering bovines ignoring the signs
in the Skydome parking lots

plopping great wet cow flops
at the Florsheimed foot of Bay Street!

Praise be to cows! for their big-boned purpose
is in keeping with goodly things

that take time   Their bulky bodies
disdain all sophistication

& if their thought be not deep
it is nonetheless wide-ranging

& though ponderous as governments
they are easily prodded by children & dogs

to shift themselves
so as not to be

a burden on the earth

Safe

1.

While I wait for the van   along comes a road
      with its terrible burden of hurry
      & sudden shatterings

While I wait for the van   along comes a forest
      of postered telephone-poles: paroled
      pedophile WANTED
      halfway living in one of these houses

While I wait for the van   along comes a man
      who trains cops in deadly force
      who knows just how many police deaths
      are caused every year by *edged weapons*

      meaning knives axes
      samurai swords   perhaps words
      of cutting

      criticism
      from mothers of dead edge-wielding
      drunks & mental patients

      who ask *Why?*   thinking
      Avoidable   knowing
      who plays it safe
      knowing full well
      who really has the edge

2.

While I wait for the van   along come the God-eyes
        of Neighbourhood Watch
        all-seeing behind parted curtains   peering
        over every hedge

        We call police   their stickers threaten
        as God calls the lightning
        down on the sinner

        & they do   because I've waited
        too long on their corner
        for my life to come
        home to roost   Suspicious
        character in my new
        safe neighbourhood   I'm one
        who will bear watching

Victorians

Theoretical city
to one without wheels   I whittle
it down to size
with pedestrian knowing

Temperance dried up these streets
in nineteen oh something
& thirst became the hidebound
neighbourhood legacy –
oasis reversed

Within the unrelenting monotony
of one flat red brick on another

the eye alights
gratefully
on small flourishes:

a fan of verticals over a window
the angling out of
corners like sharp-edged

teeth   In sweat-stained
summer drudgery
without a cold beer at hand   such
tricks were the mason's play
his material pleasure

& lasting whisper to future
generations: brick
talking about brick

Fear of wallpaper: a novena to William Morris

> Wallpaper frays, curls down in the ceiling's corners
> where the room has drawn smaller into itself
> —T. Crunk

Big locks on tiny rooms: tell-tale sign
of a former boarding-house

No blue *Fruit* no *Honeysuckle*
to commend preservation
Walls of upper hall & attic stair
muddy grey-brown   stained & bubbled:
skin disease

*   *   *

Fear of stripping
& watching
plaster come away

when papering over the cracks
has held it together
through world wars   roomers   & children
What latecomer now dares violate
such fragile membranes?

*   *   *

Short stool   Long pole
with a blade taped to it

Lean out
Find a seam &
slash   Let plaster-ash
of past lives
dust the present

*　　*　　*

Winding sheets fall over shoulders
robing me in grave clothes
Brittle worthless currency
fills my pockets

Cracks in the plaster
whisper
ragged-assed news from nowhere

*　　*　　*

Sweep up exhausted paper:
another day on the Exchange

Ticker-tape parade for the unknowns

*　　*　　*

Discovered under: historical
graffiti

Date of construction
Missionaries' signatures
Date of duplex
Doctor's signature

Chain letter
to & from OCCUPANT
one constant address
settling through time

Afraid to break
we add our names
to the people's archive
before burying it again

*   *   *

The long-dead hanger did his best
in the front attic room
where sloping walls will bend me
to my writing   Here paper
boxes me in

walls & low ceiling one seamless
abstract   mottled like
smudged fingerprints
of slaughterhouse workers
Heintzman piano tuners

CPR section men
cut back to a buck twenty
per ten-hour day

Under my feet reports
of the daily war

*   *   *

& now from beneath the lino
the yellow news:

our boys' inexorable advance   Charley
McCarthy selling Chase & Sanborn coffee
racist Sunday funnies & wrestling notices
tips on cooking liver illustrated
with photos of energetic
liver-eating dancers

vacuous housewives rhapsodic over
miracle powders & soaps
single gals & businessmen stricken
with *B.O.* halitosis
nerve troubles

society columns where every
doughboy on a weekend pass
takes a virgin
& leaves her

to act out the home-front heroine
turning collars saving slivers of soap
cheerfully awaiting her warrior

*   *   *

Unstripped living
room   Resolve to blend into
the scheme

Buy a blue couch   hang
a blue picture

become blue
animals

drifting in & out
of blue flowers

Butcher's boy

There's an art
to cutting up carcasses
If I do good floors   he'll teach me   Nothing
more beautiful
than red meat

though accidents happen
Around the meat saw daydreaming
can cost you
fingers   He laughs *Here Ma'am*
some extra
gristle & bone for the dog

His pal from the packing plant is
simple now   A frozen beef
swung down the track too fast
He was making fun of the boss
on company time
It smashed his laughter sideways
against the brick

There's a dust
brown-sugar soft
that you throw on the floor
& sweeping it up cleans the tiles
In the window corner a few have
curled & broken   *Go easy there   Mind*
you don't pull them loose

The cool display glows white
in SORRY WE'RE CLOSED darkness
I wash the rubber mats where women stand
puddling in galoshes pointing out
cuts they'd like   Pigs'
knuckles short ribs chops
He lays them out so nice

Petitioning

They're on their knees
in the precious dirt
when you come around

the people who sign
because they have little enough

the ones with far too much
zucchini   too many plums

who fill your protesting hands
with their stake in the nation

who nod & smile
& say neighbourly things
in unofficial languages

Ministry of Sleep

They haggle in the Ministry
over whether it shall be permitted
to scratch a hollow in the dirt
& sleep on a leaf   & if so
how much to tax the landowner
for *improvements*

Sleep on a stone   sleep on a leaf –
wherever one sleeps   the nightlight of
Ministry watches   regulating
the size of each stone   the number
of sleepers on each leaf   Because
each leaf & stone owes something
to government   Because
no one may sleep

in the clutch of this city without
answering to government
for the width of their burrow
the depth of their sleep

& the Ministry gloats if
neighbour should snitch against neighbour
Someone is sleeping on a leaf in the yard next door
Palms itch at word of illicit
sleeping   burn at the prospect
of hefty fines against drifters
Should a leaf owner purchase
a licence   still there are
taxes & laws   tax on
the business use of the leaf   regulations
that it fit the neighbourhood character   be made of

genuine leaf materials   to the
approved leaf plan   Because
the Ministry must be master
of all that sleeps in this   our city

reserving to itself the power to
sell the city outright
to multinationals
with monstrous sleep requirements
whose home cities were long ago twisted
by the nightmares of corporate sleeping   Oh yes
let them buy all our leaves to sleep on
because we have nothing but leaves to sell
& there's nothing we want but money

Door-to-door

In Little Rock they know
Not answering the telephone is a way of rejecting life,
That it is our business to be bothered, is our business
To cherish bores or boredom, be polite
To lies and love and many-faceted fuzziness.
              – Gwendolyn Brooks

trooping up tongue-tied heads full of knots
in woggles & short pants we're boys
scouting girls guiding peddling those nasty
cookies short-sighted witnesses
two-by-two onto the gopherwood ark of your
front porch unfunny comics
about heaven in our iron
grip our breezy apocalyptic spiel rattling on
the narrow-gauge single-track railway of faith

here we come tree-hugging
hippies with a few new
growth rings round the trunk dewy-eyed
yellow-bellied sapsucker savers paradise-
paving drain-snaking roof-patching weed
-whacking leaf-mulching dry-gulching
entrepreneurs worrying about the
crumbling foundation the spiritual eco-
nomical-illogical degradation
of life in general & yours in particular share
our worry please

hurry we know you'd care
if you'd only put down that
cold beer remote control chainsaw shotgun

please squint & print please
scrawl your worried name right here by the x
static testimonials of sexually satisfied
housewives in your area sign our
petition subscription contract blood oath covenant with
god we've taken your name in vain
off the mailbox the kraft dinner out of your mouth the
nap out of baby's bottle to do crack
-the-door-open persuasion
the chocolate-covered baseball-uniform
pitch the incendiary fanatic
unabomber lightbulbs that burn eternal
though forever's over the end's

coming like a thief in the night (book of
judas) so buy our repulsive
invader security system & we'll go away for only
five sleazy payments get all twenty-six
hardcover volumes the complete
maintenance package we've got
roofing siding weeping
tile shampoo your
conscience aluminise your kids blacktop your
wife earwax your earwig & never
water weed or seed again this little beauty can suck
up ball bearings would you believe

sign this to keep the corner church
from praying so goddamn loud buy a chance
to be hit by lightning in the j.l. borges
babylonian lottery all proceeds proceed directly
to the fathomless pocket of need you see here
from which we issue a tax amusing receipt &

a satisfied burp we want to send
deserving underprivileged kids to
boot camp or disneyworld whichever's closer
to your heart we want you to worry
late into the night about developers
toxins rape of the wilderness
& women to rile you up about vile parole-
violating-child-molesting-drunk-driving-drug-taking
gun-toting concerned citizens like yourself & the threat
to our homes posed by epidemic homelessness if this
catches on we'll all be living in shopping carts got to

nip it in the bud catch it while we can get in on
the ground floor keep our shoulders to the wheel noses
to the grindstone pedal to the metal ear
to the ground foot in the door raise it
with the ministry put a bug in their ear put it on the ballot
take it to the tallest court in the land we're short
a hundred thousand signatures can we have five
minutes of your precious time it won't take a second
it's our annual canvas for corduroy
roads our march for the legless our campout for shut-ins
our prayer group for atheists our laryngectomee
singalong our dance for death
benefits give blood or money raise
cain or awareness win rights for
lefties increase government fondling longer
money shorter sweat we've got slogans buttons
ribbons of every hue & cry an entire semiotic
ethical shorthand your name appears on the voters' list
on washroom walls on the roll up yonder your

john hancock john henry john doe joe blow
goes here john q. citizen it's a scandal a crime the
chance of a lifetime an offer you can't refuse it's the future
of your children we stand firm against oncoming traffic
the rising cost of alcohol loose dogs & morals
we encourage screaming in the houses

of parliament to ask why
welfare why day-care why one-legged
cancer patients why not the military why not
the banks why our only hope should be to consume
our way out of recession & into planetary devastation it's
clear cut if we don't cut out clear-cutting no one will
spot the spotted owl soon we'll be unspotting spotted
owls & spotting only unspotted owls in uncleared spots &
will the bottom line be uppermost in your mind how
are you this evening neighbour are you the lady of the
house the lake the harbour the immaculate conception
a landed alien citizen registered voter rented homeowner
your daddy's girl your mother's pride &
joy the only english-speaking adult in this
twelve block area aren't you
concerned about recent shocking developments on the
periphery of your peripheral vision sorry can we call back
at a more inconvenient time let us leave you
some literature that tells you everything
you never asked to know about us we are

mothers against fathers sisters against brothers twins
against cloning children against
parenthood go-getters against stop signs
money-grubbers against chicken-feed chickens against

colonel sanders sports against news nudists against weather
english against french against jerry lewis against telethons
against violence against women against patriarchy
anarchy malarkey we've cornered the market
on self-righteous indignation it's you & me against
the world & every man for himself
wild-eyed flotsam & jetsam against
the s/weeping tide of history we're
grouches against marxism reds against
bullfighting dykes against flooding chinese
against checkers abacus-makers against the computer
spiders against the worldwide web we're the buck-naked sons of
freedom & the corseted daughters of the american revolution
the children of howdy dowdy brigitte bardot
& marshall mcluhan
we're lively cranks who've been shafted a passionate
laurel&foolhardy army
a footsore public splinter
-est group of stammering
missionaries have you seen our position

on sex in public
schools with no advertising
budget we need your help to ban beauty
in the eye of the beholder & smoking
wherever there's fire help
install speed bumps on the road
to the new society forgive us
for sponging your time your attention your lousy
ten dollars forgive us for presuming
to the perennial pesky
democracy of door-to-door

Baby food for thought

Where babies come from

from out of thin air
from the gap
between finger & wedding ring

from dancing in the streets
on the day the war is over

from the fire
started by rubbing together
a woman & a man

from dream-cheques
dead relatives signed
with their given names

from recycled UN reports
on overpopulation

from the spidery basement
that covets
what's moved to make space for a nursery

from the rocking chair left
anonymously
outside the walls of Troy

Journal: late entry

I always wondered
how it would feel
to hold you   At seven weeks
my arms were as eager & long as
this!!

At eight I was
fiercely concentrated   Your
little headache weighed less
than an aspirin

These last months I've mastered
the yoga of cramped spaces

Now you're waiting   I sit
on my haunches & keep you
waiting longer

doing a final Lascaux
on the muscle walls
of my cave

Father calls at the mouth   My last
moment alone!   Don't rush me!

I fold my old clothes
gather my strength
& begin

Faith

Jesus was born in Germany
& bears the numbered tattoo to prove it
AM 841 06   It's him

you remind me of – heavy
dark head   cheeks to live off
in lean times to come
faint eyebrows   pale
lips mouthing mysteries

Like magi   strangers bend low
to whisper
Just like a doll delighting

your mother whose few
mouse-chewed
mildewed
mementoes of babyhood
bear disproportionate weight

who hears in this adoration an echo
of the one unapocryphal truth
discernible amid strike-outs   misspellings
jumbled upper- & lower-cases

in her mother's washed-out hand
on page 3 of that dime-store gospel
Baby's Own Story

Just like a doll   She reads
& re-reads the trite scripture
a Dead Sea Scroll of her own
nativity legend   as if hers

was the first mother ever to
think it & she the first child
to inspire it   My mother's

silent baby was the Word
made clay   no plastic
false prophet speaking in
mechanical tongues   One
Christmas after another
the Son of God & Koppelsdorf
lay in the church manger
bisque head   fine-painted features
a newborn pushing 90 now

& dressed in my grandfather's
christening gown   the one
we unceremoniously declined   He's the one

that makes sense for me
of your mother's unshakeable belief

that being compared to a doll
is a compliment   You resemble
that Jesus

a droopy-headed flower
with rag-soft body   dressed
in our precious histories
& faded faith

Cold snap

Pacing her sleepward   her tiny
fist clutching my chest hair

I think rabbits
how they pull out their own fur
to nest their young

how her uncle   as a kid
failed to keep them in straw

& found them one morning
frozen to the metal cage floor

                              Drunk
on breast milk   she slumps against me
warm in her first winter while   in his
the Premier

drunk on power   declares
holy war on the poor

& we find them one by one
inadequately nested
frozen in alleys   doorways
& the floors of unheated bus shelters

Spirit of Rin Tin Tin

Uncle lies minutes from death
in the snow & his dog
is barking

running back & forth   frantic
barking
barking
barking

blocking the neighbour in her driveway
– a nurse as fate would have it –
telling her over & over & over

(Will this creature never understand?
I'm saying it loud! I'm saying it clearly!
Is she foreign? Is she deaf?
Why doesn't she get it?
HE'S DYING, YOU IDIOT!)

Luckily this nurse suckled
at the tit of TV culture
& even without subtitles   recognizes
the universal doggie gesture for *Help,*

my master is trapped in an abandoned mine shaft!
the same signal that lives forever in syndication
through insomniac hours of night
which even now is studied at
the outer limits of the cosmos
by superior intelligences
trying to make sense of Earth

She is calling the ambulance now   she is calling
the Purina Pet Hall of Fame   she is calling
on Heaven itself *In the name of*
Man's best friend   in the spirit of
Lassie   Hobo   & Rin Tin Tin
save him   save us
save us all

Sweep second hand

The wind cannot be brought into the house
          – Arab proverb

A solid week of wind   The maple
shakes its keys outside the bay window

while she attends
sound-hungry   from
a nest of pillows

In her ongoing tests of the
vocal equipment she becomes
the leafwhisper

replacing yesterday's
ambulance wail
explosive laugh
pretend cough

By mid-afternoon she's transfixed
by the whoosh of
homing pigeons   Somewhere once
the world moved this way
for me   Late father   I'm guided back there
& become the grateful shadow

thrown by this tiny figure
standing close to the sun
of her wonderment   Her mother

who lost too much too soon
fears the gift

may be snatched away
How long have we got?   How long
can a good thing last?

The pigeons wheel above us –
a clock with many hands –
shadow-dappling our days
& we follow them
spinning

Baby food for thought

Fatherhood: a corner
of the basement where nails &
screws end in baby
food jars

Today   flamboyant orange
in ear-to-elbow sweet potato
she is Baby   shaping raw matter
toward distinct identity   reshaping me
toward Father   almost my father
her workshop proudly
chaotic while mine
shores up an outmoded Self
with illusions of order

Mexico   My brother
suffering the trots
cures himself eating nothing
but baby food

Father   brother   baby   me
Everyone sees the resemblance
Of course

you are what you eat   We are
that one perfect face
on each tiny jar
of one-inch finishing

Family trees

✌ Oak

They drove the two-door from Winnipeg
an oak chair wedged in the back

a piece Dad's mother saved
when the bankers took the farm

Under the butternut tree
we almost broke a leg
trying to jimmy it out

                    After
we sat on it gingerly
afraid its history
couldn't bear us

Now it stands by the phone
waiting

the oldest thing in the house

❧ Butternut

Messy tree says Mike
who cut his down years ago

He shows me his butternut stump
like it's some sort of lesson
like he gnawed it down with his teeth

It might be 150   if the arborist is right
roots fingering out below
as far as the branches above

into Mike's garden   Joan's
& on toward the church
sucking up all that holy water

A heritage tree   Not many left   Maybe
the city will save it

That fall
in our third-floor bedroom treehouse
we are planting the seed
of a daughter

& overhear Mike
cursing us under his breath

fiercely sweeping
our fruitfulness from his driveway

a Belgian Job
afflicted by plagues & trials
he doesn't deserve
When butternuts hit trashcans
it sounds like it's raining stones

Dreams of the spoon

A stay-home father dreams of the spoon
the medicine spoon of fever time
the smashed-against-glasses musical spoon
the catapult spoon of mashed bananas

His cartoon-colonized dreams prove the spoon
batters all thought to pablum
scoops out his eyes gone mole-blind
in the sun of worldly ambition
craters his heart — that
ungrateful stone —
from the bruised fruit of his body

It glows in his hand   All night
he tunnels with it toward China
By sandbox spoonfuls
he eats his hungry way out
boring through the earth's core

or he sharpens it surreptitiously
against the harsh walls of his cell
till the handle's a shiv
or a lock-pick his ticket
out of this toy Alcatraz

He becomes the spoon   the un-
silver spoon the less privileged are born with
pitted by acids of baby spit
bitten by iron-grip milk teeth

He's offered up to her & licked clean
every day of their life together
washed like a third hand & left

gleaming dully
in the drainboard dark

a sleepless   child-minding
night-light moon
in her infant sky

Vertical society

In a garden eyeblink   pencil-size zucchini
turns Louisville Slugger
So tipsy sitter transforms
into upright citizen

leaning out for toys
locating balance point   discovering
gravity – testimony to
instinctive experimental intelligence –
Galileo in Pisa dropping
cannonballs off the tower

Standing at last amazed
on handgrips of old green father
she rocks   bounces   testing
the jerry-rigged bone
& ligament limits

of her short membership
in vertical society   Not yet
a taxpayer   not yet a vote
to be bought   not old enough
to survive

on the government's welfare diet
of gluestarch & dented tinned tuna   One leg
describes an arc   indecision

in motion   asking
quicksand?   landmines?
tiger traps?   crumbling
infrastructure?

chooses for a moment
safety – one foot atop the other
More puzzling then
to escape this wobbly impasse

much bending & flexing
light-stepping back & forward
stroke-patient staggers into stances
too wide   too narrow   Suddenly

boldness   curiosity   impatience rise
giant in her   *Screw the Premier!*
She executes five
beautiful balanced steps   This
is the start of something &
no turning back

On her own two feet
she needs me no longer
than a gliding-back dance partner's
heartpang   Her progress
is my retreat   One day she'll run
from my outstretched arms   taller

than her short parents   taller than
the short-sighted Premier
& his short-tempered Government
of Punishment   The old uterus
that pushed her out
will be the last withered birth
-day balloon   She'll wear her shrunken parents
in her ears & forget

where those faint inner voices
are coming from   In the movies
the wounded one always says

Leave me   I'll hold them off
buy you some time

I start rehearsing   even ad libbing
having found my motivation   Those lines already
just a few pages away

I can't go on   I'd only slow you down
If there's any beauty in the future
come back for me

One is one but two is four

The devil will count
every straw
if you hang a broom behind her door

By then it's morning
& no harm's come to her

Caring's arithmetic
as calculated elsewhere

Or:

Let her feet never touch the ground
(let n *be the number of months)*
This keeps her from being
snatched back   She's
not yet a being
of this earth

                        But for
this nuclear family   how to figure
carrying capacity   tally
the charge it can bear before
exploding?

Parkbenched   Unsolicited envy
from harried mother of twins   *One*
is one she reckons but *two is four*

We no sooner had *xx*
than folks began asking
what comes after 1   We hand them
a broom & say
You do the math

Loyalty management

The little engine of my days un-
nests the nesting cups yellow
red blue yellow red blue
smaller to bigger   so fast
Doesn't need me
for this   I winnow

the mail: letter with surreal poem
plane tickets   consumer survey
asking if we suffer

dandruff   & what is the family
income?

Lunch   Peas
in her hair   occasionally
her mouth   In the poem
Stalin's brain gets fed
to a large snake   Sated
she naps

while we stroller to the store for more
milk   Have we ever bought
Head & Shoulders?   Home again

check the ticket fine print   *insurance
declined*   Father's birthday
unmissable   Those once-in-a-blue-moon
heart-tug visits will be
leaky-heart-valve visits now   sped up
like a racing pulse

to every few octogenarian/baby-months   But
the family income?   These

tickets paid for with years

of shrink-the-world Air Miles   *Woe*
the world is tiny in the brochures

& mailed (return address says) from the
Loyalty Management Group   She
wakes   demands her share
of mail   starts shredding the questionnaire

There are no edges to my loving now
as torn questions & forced-choice answers
come snowing from her hands
to dandruff her dark hair

To the kingdom

Seizing *key* by the tail
& *Da* by the shorthairs

of eyebrow & beard
she yanks the world up by its root

-sounds   Consciousness leaps
everywhere at once like
bushy-tailed *swirrls* in the butternut

starvation-scrounges the spilled
seed-corn of parentspeech

kisses like a priest
the bible of nursery stories
with its Holy Trinities
of pigs   bears   gruff goats

Co Ein! Co Ein!   Suddenly
we're all invited

the whole creation welcomed
now that the key is in her hands

Fame

My fifteen minutes is here   in this
half-hour-later-in-Newfoundland neighbourhood
just off the edge
of the world that really matters

Celebrity in No Frills
the diaper ghetto of Shopper's Drug
playing low-rent Bojangles
to Baby's Shirley Temple

While the President acts
presidential   bombing someone
through stains on a woman's dress

we buy twenty-four cats
in the Stale Cereal & Pet Food aisle
of High Value Discount Variety
where Shirley's broken English fits right in

then it's on to cheese buns   where
if it's the doting one
she may partake of the gracious
cookie sacrament   How precious
are the faithful in the sight of
God & small business!

Afternoons   Wednesday or Friday
we drop in at Drop-in

Monday Tuesday & Thursday   it's
geese or the swings   If
it's raining   a dry
library hello   After years of
walk-ons   at last
a small speaking part

in an *Our Town* knock-off   wooden lines & no
direction   At this rate   how long till *Days*
of Our Circumscribed Lives?   Supreme
Justices opine on how best to break up
the nation   I chip in 2¢ worth
on buggies & banks with steps

My father's pocket watch

What was my father saying?
He was wishing me luck, he was saying love in a language
That has no word for it, the language of fathers and sons.
— Thomas McGrath

Calls it a turnip   Weeks after
they x-ray his heart   I'm showing off
our newborn & he slips
it into my hand saying
he's had it forever

Its name is Pilot   Never cared
for a ticking wrist shackle but this
is different   a heavy
palm-sized

medallion of family time
a live thing baby wants
to kiss   This is heartbeat
history

running
him   to me   to her
I baby it all the way home
where it suddenly

stops   hands
together over its face

I shake it   first gently
then fiercely   *Sweet*
Jesus don't
die on me now

Its worn jewels weep
blue minutes
Gap-toothed wheels
feel them trickling out
The sadness of the watch

shakes me first gently
then fiercely

Wound tight   it starts up
runs on again
in progressively-shorter bursts
Something tells me

this is our future:
running
stopping
shaking

Let the sun never fall into the hands of government

Ministry of Edges
for Olga

> Why a Ministry of the Interior? There *is* no Interior.
> There ought to be a Ministry of Edges.
> > – Canadian ex-patriot

Where is the interior of a knife?

Twenty-six hundred miles long
never more than a tenth as wide
The serrated edge of Chile
a rough blade that has slit many throats

One morning in '73
you board the bus for work
& the driver   with something in his voice
says *I wouldn't if I were you*   Leaving him
the fare you turn home   pack a bag
while the Ministry arrives at your office
searching

& at your friend's door   they've come for her
but neglected to bring a photo   Straight-faced
she tells them   *Sorry*
she's not here

Even now there's a plan in a bottom drawer
at the Ministry of Edges
patiently awaiting its next moment:
this one will flatten the unions
this one in charge of razor wire
certain papers to be shredded
cables to cut

& there will be no interior
to vanish into   Once again you'll need to

squeeze through a narrow window
slip over an edge
to the broad ocean   some
wider country

while the Ministry prowls up & down
the length of the nation
its hunters thin &
bloodless as face cards
sniffing for your scent on the wind
sifting sand for your exile's tears

& thousands of miles away   you'll be
reading   dreaming   plotting return
living an interior life
in some vast canada of the mind

Green buckets

Nibbled by milk teeth of flower-water
bled by fangs of vampire weather

row on row of old wooden buckets
rot by the graveyard gate

Memory vessels consumed
from within & without

Tiers of disillusioned colour
prison green

a green with all but the green
salutation censored out

the green of whitewash

a green enfeebled by countless grief-seasons
the green of persistent vanishment

the green of spring meadows
leaching to desert nitrates

the green of the playing field
of *Estadio Chile*
where the rounded-up
hunched in the bleachers
asking *What's the score?*

the green of green-is-dying
locker room screams

the green of soon-to-be-disappeared identities
flaking apart like fake IDs

their green features fading
in bland broad daylight –
Polaroids in reverse

In the General Cemetery

... Francis Phelan became aware
that the dead, even more than the living
settled down in neighbourhoods.
　　　　　　－ William Kennedy

As in the living city   the streets of the dead
bear historic names like *Bernardo O'Higgins*

though in such ranks   each address affects
the permanence of a bank:
square stone box with iron gates
rocksolid social position

even an unlikely
bronze angel   like a winged milkman
tapping timidly at the door of someone
especially pious   The disappeared

are not so elaborately housed
or so whimsical   Only their killers know
in which safe deposit
landfill their broken bodies lie dumped
never to be claimed
the twin keys of banker & client
conveniently lost   They sleep not in family vaults

but in a blood kinship of resistance
where neighbourhood is an alphabetical
accident   Only their incorporeal names
ages & dates of detention remain
incorruptible on the white stone
ledger of the dead

one of few substantial acts of memory
in a nation of studied forgetting

The last Chileans

Slapped together from scrounged materials
the *media aguas* on your block
live up to their name when the rains
quagmire their earthen floors

they become
half water   breeding pools of
poverty's customary contagions –
tuberculosis
envy
revolution

Yours is the highest street on the slope
till money elbows past   One morning you wake to
jagged crowns of glass
privatizing the mountains
The city's climbing club
disbands & goes home

Invisible neighbours slither out
behind tinted windshields   Impossible
even to glimpse their mansions from the street
Past the iron gates & guards we only imagine
sky-blue pools   the scotch & water
You dub them the last Chileans: above them
only the Andes & the border

Property

At the end of the road   urchin children
squat in the dirt & shit
on private property

From their dung   cactus & thistle grow
a community to hold
the vacant legal ground

& the Ministry of Fences quakes & rumbles
a Richter 7   an 8
trying to shake the poor
off the back of the earth

but thistle will not be thrown off
cactus will not be parched out
Their tough roots knit
the cracked dry land together

The Question Building

This blunt puzzle palace
squats like a Sphinx
a black hole of silence
on the noise-edge of your neighbourhood

a Chilean interrogative
bracketed with question marks:
¿Qué pasó aquí?

Nondescript   yet somehow
conspicuous
in its abandonment

No one brings mail – has it ever
owned up
to an address?

No child dares peek through
a crack to find
monster shapes
in the floor's brown stains

To tear it down would admit
ownership of its history
& expose its deadbolted rooms
to the light of day

Windows boarded   it stares
eyeless like a torture victim

or a general
inscrutable behind shades
wordless in the months before the coup
the wafer of future betrayal
heavy as stone on his tongue

Rumour has it
last rites were given here
without benefit of clergy
                Confessions
& teeth
extracted without dentist or anaesthesia

Tell the truth – you'd like to pry into this
innocuous box of held breath
sweep out its dark corners   scour
its drains where the night wind
whispers *Give up*
your secrets

You ask yourself which curious
cop in your English class
might have sought answers here

which hand now raised to the teacher
might not have been so open
or so empty

The growing middle class

In this vertical society the middle class is
the living

No class indisputably lower
than the buried   burned &
drowned   none more
unreachably upper than
the shadowy *momios* who slip

white gloves of self-granted amnesty
over unclean hands   trailing the stink
of scorched flesh behind them
rustling a chorus of disappeared voices
in the silk of their tailored suits

Between these extremes   the middle
-men & -women of small appliances
newer cars   good schools
Why dig up the past? they ask

*Life's getting better   It's comfortable
above ground*   though at every step
a well-shod foot may break through
the undermined earth

& sink in black rivers
of blood   black rivers of
justice deferred

Torturer's dream

In the precipice city
of Valparaíso   I am climbing
the endless stairs

bearing a beaten body   a skin-sack
of broken twigs   my shoulders
prayer-shawled with its
purple & yellow flowers

& all the while it speaks   *Don't I*
know you?   How's
the family?   Didn't I
once date your sister?

There's something obscene
in such presumption   What
malice informs this
relentless needling?   As if the physical
burden weren't exhausting enough ...

Maddened to desperation   a brute
beast suffering flies   I would
smash the mouth into silence
were the body not already
dead   A man in my position
doesn't plead for mercy

yet somehow we're bound & I'm
powerless to shake free
We are rescued

& rescuer   alone in our burning
building   bride & bridegroom on
the threshold of a new life   Christ
& cross climbing toward
inevitable Calvary

It's clear we will never escape
our incendiary embrace   never
enter the nuptial bedroom   There's
no hope of resurrection   only

perpetual crucifixion
the wood   the flesh   each
born to this marriage   yet cursing
our luck & each other   imagining
softer   less obstinate lives
that might have been ours

Mote sin mote

Sold on the street by the dipperful
through hot summer afternoons
a distinctive Chilean refreshment
mote con huesillo

or *mote* for short: peach nectar
with barley kernels

& if *huesillo* is the shrunken
sun-dried peach
sunk to the bottom of its own juices

just as a weighted human body
dropped into the sea
sinks & rots till
there's no face or fingerprint

then the child's request for *mote
sin mote* really means *hold the kernels*
which briefly float
suspended in thick liquid
like the few last teeth
when all flesh has fallen away

Sexpresso

Downtown they've crossbred
the café & the peep show   Men pay
to lean on a rail while women fetch
coffee

High-heeled   in minis & low-cut blouses
or chiffon-over-bustier   they sashay
to & from the machine
bearing tiny cups   smiling
making male small talk
feel bigger

They don't dance or strip   There's
no touching   They have only
the same few steps
in which to swivel the hips   give a toss
of the head   a coy look   They refine
the smallest motions down to
microns of hinted intimacy   flit
within a birdcage of allure

There are no chairs   Men come
& go in minutes   No alcohol
No food   There is only
one hunger

The Ministry of Bitter Pleasures controls
how it looks from the street
Mini-skirts: clear glass   Tinted if the style is
boudoir   The customers are all business
types   their fingernails are clean   They assess
the asses   hoping to get what they like

When the waitress smiles   they smile   pretending
the place has an ocean view & pie like Mom's
They go because so few longings
can be stirred with a coffee spoon

The Snow Hotel

In the Snow Hotel   money washes itself
by passing from hand to hand

the grubbier it gets
the cleaner it is
the more soiled & used
the more innocent

The mayor swings open the door with a bow
Senators fall to their knees
clutching shoeshine rags

From over the border   money comes
to sleep on crisp white linen
to take the steam   stretch naked on
cedar benches   slip down
into the whirlpool of the Snow Hotel

As it lies there
blood-stains fade   the smell
of gunpowder dissipates

With every ablution the shoulders of the Snow Hotel
unhunch themselves   till the building stands taller
than any on the skyline
taller than the Andes

& money goes home from vacation
refreshed   virginal
ready for anything
& the welcome is always the same:
You look like a million!

The message

> No, she cried, no, thus inventing a word with a future
> — Günter Grass

1988: a chink appears
in the armour-plate of government

a hairline fracture through which
daylight's visible

Through this mouth people shout
one word in many voices
through this paper-thin slot they post
their written verdict

Fleets of diesels are needed
to haul the immense tonnage
of *N*s & *O*s

an Andes of syllable-pebbles
blocks out the sun

The message's dirt-poor simplicity
baffles the General   He reads it
over & over in stunned disbelief

as if it might change
as if it were not too late

It is too late   Each blacklung-letter
shallows his breath further
His hands grow palsied unfolding
what looks like a love note but isn't

Each message is a grain of silt
clogging the arteries of his heart
a steadily-thickening cataract
in each dimming eye
He shivers to consider
its grave purpose

He wonders where he might have heard
its blunt sound before
Was it the footfall of someone
led away to be shot

the anguished denial of a
lover   a parent   a child

Was it this the dead were singing
when they still had tongues

the noise they screamed in answer
to all the electric questions?

It saved no one then
yet becomes for them now
the utterly perfect word

a word small enough to slip
like a letter bomb through this
tiny crack in history   a word
worthy of its every
emphatic repetition

a common
redemptive word
the life-affirming negative

plain as bread
hard as stone
pure as water

a word with a future

Bright New Year

Dragging our troubled history   we
surrender & walk empty-handed
into the night   On the sand
strangers dance out of reach
of the pounding surf   A radio
blasts out the hits   There are magnums

of champagne & a hopeful
if weak-willed democracy   We count down
the last seconds in one nostalgic
demo of solidarity

& the sky opens fire   Popped corks
shoot wildly into the shadows
Dark figures agitate
the year's baptismal spirit
spraying the meagre crowd
like toy water cannon

Domestic life of the torturer

He dreads the closet
where sometimes he sees
men hanging   To make them
suits again   he forces
his hands into their wounds

At Mass   his heart is
an airless cathedral
where *Our Father*s die
without echo   the holy wafer
an unmelting stone in his mouth
He has no spit   no prayers   cannot make
confessions   The crucified man looks
too familiar   He does not go back

Evenings he watches his daughter undressing
her Barbies   He gives up
smoking for fear
he'll stub out on a breast

In a dream   his senile father bends over him
in uniform   touching him with shocking
tenderness   Before the day is out
he has the old man committed

Home from work early   he blunders in
on his wife   naked   bound
with velvet ropes   being
spanked by a neighbour

Smiling
she confesses
He knows when to stop

The General as civilian

He braves the brash sun
of democracy unrepentant
brazenly take the host
in his gleaming mouth

He grows paunchy
wears a Sunday suit
becomes Senador
or abuelo   evades

judgement by pleading
frailty   The black leather
hair whitens   the muscles
go slack   Yet the old man
holds his faithful as closely
as grandchildren on his knee
His unswerving conviction
makes his very name
a sheathed claw

Though his fingernails are clean   he knows
where all the bodies are buried   Years
of warm breakfast muffins with secret police
makes the testicle-squeezing pliers no more
to him

than sugar tongs on the tea tray
a ruined body no more than
a drowned midge
skimmed from the orange juice

The Forces of Arms & Order
are a kind of family
business   from which
Granddad is officially
retired   In the backyard he stakes out
his shadow on a generous chain

feeds it phone books   communion wafers
& the broken bones of enemies
whose marrow goes on nourishing
his illegitimate children

Roadkill

Desert   glacier   whatever else might lie
buried   or in wait
the extremes of Chile stretch far beyond
the apron strings of day trips   Couldn't
rent a car 'cause I never mastered
the standard   *Bloody or burned?* Over barbeque
a friend of a friend says he'll teach me

It's New Year's Day – sloshed red & resolutions
Round & round the block I
shift & lurch & stall
while great hunks of meat sizzle
& blacken on the grill   Fixed on the stick
my peripheral vision narrows   Wherever I turn
the pedestrian limit of my understanding
darts out in front of me   I fear
his calling it a crash course was no accident

Small wonders

> Not only humans longed for liberation.
> All ecology groaned for it also. The revolution
> is also one of lakes, rivers, trees, animals.
> — Ernesto Cardenal

❧ Eucalyptus seedpods

Little diving bells
in which the tree-idea
sinks to the far floor of the world
& waits to grow back to open air

Loosed with a prayer   the seeds
in the pod's tiny chapel-heart
leave it incised with a sign of the cross

Biomass liberation theology
redolent with incense

⁎ Pine cone

Shut tight: a jeweller's
past midnight
in a tough neighbourhood

Rough touch:
a pocket pineapple
harsh pinprick scales

Armoured seeds
Arboreal hand-grenade

Stone-hard   Intense
as though concentrating
an entire tree
in hostile conditions

Symmetry distorted
by grotesque swelling
one side of the base

like some hyper-developed lobe
of the seed brain
obsessing

❧ Granaries of dawn
for Emma

Flying toward sunrise & the nuzzle-warmth of you
my travel-treasures are the scattered
seed corn of morning –

pine cone   odd bit of
shell from Neruda's beach   still-fragrant
seedpods of eucalyptus – Nature's broadcast
pocket silver
magpied together for you

to keep in a box of Chilean redwood
from *Los Graneros del Alba*   where many
reckon their artisan life from
the year of the coup

& lonelier now than ever
as dark clouds pinken & suffuse with light
I vow never to wander so far again
from *mi cielito*   my little sky

A dream, a wake

The creatures

Caged in your sleep   may the great beasts
bless & protect you always   the bears of
loving kindness   the wise Blakean tigers
of wrath & the horses of
instruction   Dream untroubled
by paradox of proportion – the ladybug
bigger than the cat   the mouse
as large as the elephant
& wearing pants   In their all-forgiving silence
may they love you in ways we fail to
these friends of first refuge
the peaceable kingdom
where the lion lies down with the lamb

Mister P.

Oh the small afflictions
In the heart of toys!
...
Oh cemetery of Childhood
Reveal your secret light
    – Joaquim Cardozo

His silence is absolute
oracular

A master criminal
mocking the police
his features change
with each new witness

His body & mind are one
He smells of the earth

As he withers & shrinks
his magic grows more powerful

Approaching death his gaze
intensifies   He sprouts
long white eyes
looks far into the future

until he is given up utterly
to visions
& becomes all eyes
a small down-cellar god

A pet

A severed hand lives
in a glass cage

Hairy   Dark
It feeds on the blood
of live crickets

Set down inches
from its skulking corner
their scrape-song
takes on a frantic edge

their silences thicken with prayers
for a last-minute call from the governor

At the end of each lifetime the hand
flips onto its back & wriggles
an hour or two

working out of itself
as though taking leave
of a glove

& when at last it's shiny & shy
a debutante again

the ghost of the old self remains
to remember it by

Wally's Smoke

> I am tangled in the net of the world
> – Wang Wei

The fist of March fell on a Monday   I'm not sure
this is a typo   When I walked by the shop
called Wally's Smoke   I'd been reading Elie Wiesel
& it didn't seem funny   Lines of Jews
still ate spoonfuls of snow
off each other's shoulders

At the Smithsonian
Laurel's shown her half-cube & left
to her research
I finally discovered the bathroom
she wrote me later
through 'The Origins of Western Culture'
& turn right

My daughter says the sun
eats the colour off cities   I told her
that sounded just about right to me

I used to guide my life by the warnings on labels
Pain relief said *Keep out of reach of children*
Peach yogurt advised me to *Watch for pits*
Greek chocolate counselled *Keep away from bad smells*

Now I'm webbed in marriage
fatherhood & a house that makes my wife sneeze
When I met her my heart was loaded
without the safety on   Our proper clothes
intertwined them sleeves as we danced

In the underworld

Pickled fingers & eyeballs
in cloud-filled jars

Stopped clocks

Webs & old iron

It's cold   Near the furnace
a fat white ball
of babies

The floor's too spicy
for naked feet

When I slammed the door with no handle
I knew I would die

My father refused to let me

I fell up
crushing weeds

Tree of stones

You shall love your crooked neighbour
With your crooked heart
                              – W. H. Auden

It's raining stones on the neighbour's
tin roof   God's all-night punishment
for hardening our hearts & refusing
to axe the butternut

Masked bandits drowse all day
in its branches   then steal
down at night   chew the ankle
-deep blow-up pool

crash the trash & with clever leather
hands assess the night's remains
like garbage journalists
stripping us naked   spilling
our eating habits
credit history
birth control methods
to the far fence

where   near dawn   the stars pull in
behind the Church of Abundant Life
& face their doubles in wardrobe
trying to recall which self will be shot
first   Why now? Why here?
Location location location ...

Bogus public dreams
& the litter of the private
mesh gears at the fence   Tell me again
gaffer

how backlot spacemen dressed
in tin-foil
faked the moon

Waking

❧ Attic windows

Eye-level with song   How loud this blue
prairie sky

to the tremble-bird nested
in an attic shoebox

with its child's bed
its stifling storms
& three small holes
punched in for air

on my first fatherless morning in the world

❧ The farm

With a team of greys
he muscles the moon into place
In that worn yellow light
the farm is still his
to suffer for

There are 'hoppers
drought   a mortgage
I offer to write him a cheque

from the bank where labour is saved
by household gadgets   He snorts
& tells me I'm so damn smart
I'm stupid   I can hardly understand him

with that bit between his teeth
He twists his guts in fierce hands
as though wringing sweat from a shirt

❧ Griefwork

if death –
a general mailing –
should reach a household

apologize

at time of death over
eighty-seven decisions
need to be made

quickly   there is
little time

do something
every day do nothing
the first year

we did things   a flurry
of doing   guilt
over all we'd not done
& wouldn't
stick around to do

later she phoned asking
what to do   ticked off
that we'd failed
to tick off
what we'd done   list

o list   in witness whereof
I have hereunto set my hand
last

will   true copy   give &
bequeath   this body
to the beneath

all my estate
both real & surreal
for her own use
absolutely

their lawyer ensconced in his paper
explosion mouthing
coffin courtesies

fine gentleman must be hard
I know everything
difficult now your file right
here I am only
a phone call

away prepaid contract drives us
a hundred yards
to the church   fine
print   execu-tricks
money changes
everything

his Vital Statistical end
triggers oxymoronic
Death Benefit from
the Ministry of Cold Comfort

receiving
line family
plot in deepest
sympathy tears

gratefully declined thank
hospital half-staff lovingly
remembered to sit
the house so thieves
browsing obits
don't steal her blind
while we bury our dead

neighbours how christian
miracle food
to feed the multitude

these things eternal   death
& taxes   tea
& bickies

⁋ He naps in his former bedroom

Makeshift atticsleep   feet
between sheet
-music & some cobbler's
wooden shoon

commemorative spoons white
neckless Os of button collars
fine bone china silver
dollars

heirloom glass &
faded flags
before-your-time quilts
(Old Sod rags)

a steamer trunk   & wedged under
sloping wall   his bunk
tight fit   a narrow shelf
for narrow self

in father-fashioned
mother-furnished hidey-hole
another dusty rack
for antique bric-a-brac

Homemade puppet
he's jerked back
to grieve & dream
beneath the Union Jack

to bear into the future
features now deceased
to find himself
laid out pretty in the past
making his museumpeace

ᴇ Ashes to ashes

The morning he became ashes
my late father sat on the bed
cross-legged   reading the paper
I held out my hand & said *Sorry
you're dead*   He shook it
then looked at Mother
as if to ask *Who's this?*
His grip was dry

soft & yielding with occasional
bumps of bone   The fog
of confusion never enveloped him
in life but here the news was fresh
& engrossing while his past
had already burned

                    The heft
as I lowered him into the ground
brought back the deep cradle

& the weight of my daughter
newly born

~ Zero

Add up his words about
marriage & fatherhood
they'd come in the end

to zero   I spent years
floating like a bubble
on that reticence

Now the world is out of true
but place a level on his life
& the bubble lies
dead
centre

To inherit
his wise example
how else but to hold
my wife & child

On each forehead   my kiss
presses a tiny zero

❧ Old dog

We don't have a dog, but we sit this one now & then. Arthritic, afraid of thunder. It tortures him to climb stairs. Spends most of his day on another level. From the third floor, I hear his chain jingle. The sky's gone dark, the first weak drops hit the pane. Then the hard click of nails, more rattle of chain, as he hauls himself up to my room. The shakes take him over; he hangs on, lonely & scared. *Are you going to die?* I ask. No response. I can't bear more death just now. I sing softly, touch his shoulder. His dandelion fur comes loose in my hand. As the storm passes over, I whisper the threadbare comforts I never unpacked. *It's all right. Don't worry. I'm here. You rest now.*

Notes

In the poem "Loyalty management," the first line alludes to the children's story *The Little Engine That Could*. "Woe the world..." is from Hans Magnus Enzenberger, and "There are no edges..." is from Rumi.

The section title *Let the sun never fall into the hands of government* is a line from Chilean poet Clemente Riedemann.

"In the General Cemetery" makes reference to Bernardo O'Higgins, who fought for Chilean independence. A major street in Santiago is named after him.

"Ministry of Edges," "The message," and "The granaries of dawn" incorporate details of recent Chilean history. On Sept. 11, 1973 General Augusto Pinochet led a military coup against the elected socialist government of Salvador Allende. Thousands of leftists and suspected sympathizers were arrested, tortured, executed, or forced into exile. Many went underground, taking on new identities and adopting new livelihoods.

In 1988, Pinochet lost a plebiscite aimed at extending his presidency. A return to democracy followed, though an amnesty law limited legal recourse for human rights violations committed under his regime. When these poems were begun in 1998, Pinochet was still head of the armed forces, and he later became senator for life. Despite national and international efforts to bring him to trial, he avoided trial on the grounds of ill-health for years, and died December 10, 2006.

In "The Question Building," the Spanish *¿Qué pasó aquí?* means *What happened here?*

"The growing middle class" uses the word *momios* (mummies), a popular term to describe upper-class Chileans resistant to social and political change.

"The Snow Hotel" is the nickname of a posh Santiago hotel widely believed to be operated by foreign drug dealers to launder profits from the cocaine trade.

In "Wally's Smoke," the line "my heart was loaded/ without the safety on" owes a debt to a line from André Breton.

Acknowledgements

Versions of some of these poems first appeared in *The Antigonish Review*, *The Dalhousie Review*, *Descant*, *Fiddlehead*, *Gaspereau Review*, *Nimrod*, *Our Times* and *Rohwedder*. Thanks to the editors of those journals.

An early version of "Ministry of Sleep," titled "City Council Grapples with the Housing Crisis," was published in the Pulp Press anthology *More Than Our Jobs*.

The section *Let the sun never fall into the hands of government* is for Moses & Olga, with thanks. Under the title *Ministry of Edges*, some poems from that section were Honourably Mentioned by the judges of the 1999 League of Canadian Poets chapbook contest (Anne Szumigalski, Steven Michael Berzensky and Brenda Niskala), and later published by Tall Tree Press.

Thanks to *Arc*, Brick Books, Mosaic Press, *New Quarterly*, Wolsak and Wynn, and the Ontario Arts Council for financial assistance during the writing of various parts of this book.